SUSIE BROOKS

LET'S MAKE ART

BY PRINTING & STAMPING

Published in paperback in Great Britain in 2019 by Wayland

Copyright © Hodder and Stoughton, 2016

ISBN: 978 1 5263 0046 1
10 9 8 7 6 5 4 3 2 1

Printed in Dubai

MIX
Paper from
responsible sources
FSC® C104740
FSC
www.fsc.org

Wayland
An imprint of
Hachette Children's Group
Part of Hodder and Stoughton
Carmelite House
50 Victoria Embankment
London EC4Y 0DZ

An Hachette UK Company
www.hachette.co.uk
www.hachettechildrens.co.uk

Editor: Elizabeth Brent
Design: nicandlou

CONTENTS

Ragbag Robots p.8-9

Splat -a- Caterpillar p.14-15

Spots and Stripes p.16-17

Leafy Lions p.6-7

LET'S MAKE ART!

IF YOU WANT TO MAKE GREAT PICTURES QUICKLY, PRINTING AND STAMPING IS A BRILLIANT WAY TO START. YOU DON'T NEED TO SIT AND WONDER WHAT TO DRAW, JUST PRINT A SHAPE AND SEE WHERE IT TAKES YOU!

WHAT YOU NEED

You can print with almost anything - as long as you can wash the paint off afterwards! Rummage around in your school bag, fridge and kitchen drawers for things that have interesting shapes.

In this book we'll print with leaves, bottle tops, pen lids, balloons, vegetables and lots more. Check your recycling for old envelopes or card that you can use as a background for your work.

FOR THE PROJECTS IN THIS BOOK IT HELPS TO HAVE THE FOLLOWING BASIC ART SUPPLIES:

- ✓ ready-mix paints
- ✓ paintbrushes
- ✓ sponges
- ✓ coloured ink pads
- ✓ a pencil and rubber
- ✓ felt-tip pens
- ✓ scissors
- ✓ glue
- ✓ plain white paper or card
- ✓ coloured paper or card, including black
- ✓ wool, ribbon or string
- ✓ bubble wrap
- ✓ a hole punch
- ✓ kitchen paper
- ✓ newspaper

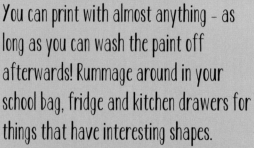

HANDY HINTS

Before you start, lay down plenty of newspaper to protect the surface you're working on.

Keep a bowl of water, a cloth and an old towel nearby to clean the objects you've been printing with. Kitchen paper is useful for wiping, too.

It can take a few goes to make a perfect print. Try these tips:

- cover the object evenly with paint - a sponge is useful for doing this

- press the object firmly down on the paper and KEEP IT STILL to avoid smudging

- lift the object straight up again afterwards, holding down the paper with your other hand.

Always wait for your print to dry before painting or sticking on details.

Sometimes printed paper wrinkles as it dries. Don't worry - you can flatten it later under a pile of books.

When you see this LOGO, you might want to ask an adult to help.

LEAFY LIONS

A LEAF—PRINTED MANE IS PERFECT FOR THE KING OF THE JUNGLE!

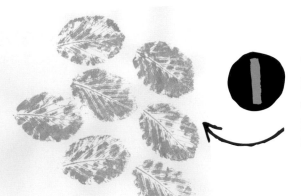

1 You can use any medium-to-large leaf for this. Cover the veiny side with orange paint and press it on to yellow paper. Add more paint and repeat. You'll need about nine leaf prints.

EARS

HEAD

2 When the prints are dry, cut them out. Arrange them in a flower shape like this:

THERE ARE TEMPLATES ON P.30 IF YOU NEED THEM!

TAIL

BODY

3 Cut out the lion's head, body, ears and tail from another piece of yellow paper. The head should fit in the middle of your leaves, with room around the edge.

WHY NOT MAKE A MULTI-COLOURED MANE?

GLUE ON THE EARS, THEN PAINT THE MIDDLE OF THEM PINK.

PAINT ON A FACE.

4 Glue the lion's body to the bottom of a large sheet of paper. Stick the leaves on top, then stick the head in the middle of the leaves.

GLUE ON THE TAIL. YOU COULD STICK ANOTHER LEAF PRINT TO THE END OF IT!

RAGBAG ROBOTS

PRINT A RABBLE OF ROBOTS USING HOUSEHOLD BITS AND BOBS!

BOTTLE TOPS

Look around your home for things that could be interesting to make prints of. Here are some ideas. Practise making prints on some rough paper first.

FORK

STAPLES, PENCIL SHARPENERS AND PEN LIDS

POTATO MASHER

SLOTTED SPATULA

WIGGLY PASTA

RIM OF MARGARINE TUB

TRY A ROBOT!

Decide which shapes would suit different parts of a robot, then print them together on a sheet of white paper.

ADD DETAILS USING SMALLER ITEMS.

START WITH THE HEAD AND BODY.

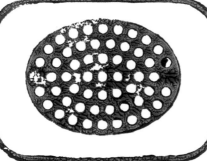

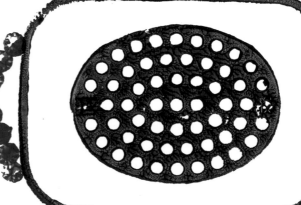

TRY A ROBOT DOG!

BOTTOM
OF EGG BOX

LOLLY STICK

PRINT SMALL
CIRCLES INSIDE
LARGER ONES TO
MAKE A DIAL.

BOTTOM OF A
PLASTIC DRINKS
BOTTLE

THIS
ROBOT'S FEET
AND HANDS WERE
PRINTED WITH THE
SIDES OF A STICKY—
TAPE DISPENSER.

END OF A RUBBER,
PRINTED SEVERAL
TIMES IN A ROW

Hello,
Mr Fork
Feet!

9

BOTTLE-TOP BALLOONS

YOU COULD PRINT THESE ON A PIECE OF FOLDED PAPER TO MAKE A GREAT GREETINGS CARD!

1 Collect the lids of some old bottles, all of a similar size. Cover the top of a lid in paint and print it on to white paper. Repeat using the other lids and different colours, to create a bright bunch of balloons!

2 Use a felt-tip pen to draw some strings coming down from the balloons.

3 Press your thumb into paint or a coloured ink pad to print a person dangling from the balloons.

DRAW ON ARMS, LEGS, A FACE AND HAIR!

4 Experiment with different balloons! Print a row of small bottle tops to make a long balloon.

TRY PRINTING WITH THE RIM OF A BOTTLE TOP, THEN FINGERPRINT SOME DOTS INSIDE!

tip

You could dangle an animal from your balloons. Make two thumbprints in the same colour. Then draw on a face, ears, legs and an elephant's trunk or a monkey's curly tail.

UH-OH, HERE COMES A BIRD TO POP THE BALLOONS!

VEGGIE JAM

CREATE A TRAFFIC JAM OF VEHICLES WITH VEGETABLE–PRINT WHEELS!

ONION

MUSHROOM WITH THE STALK REMOVED

1 Ask an adult to help you cut vegetables to give a flat surface. Dry the surface with kitchen paper, dip it in paint and practise making some prints like these.

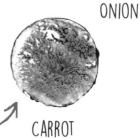

CARROT

THERE ARE TEMPLATES ON P.31 IF YOU NEED THEM!

2 For a car like this, print two mushroom wheels. Cut a piece from half a pepper to print the roof.

3 When the prints are dry, draw the car's outline and colour it in.

CUT A RECTANGLE OF POTATO TO PRINT WINDOWS LIKE THIS.

4 For a bus, start with three onion-print wheels and let them dry. Draw the outline, then add some windows.

THESE PEOPLE BEGAN AS SMALL CARROT PRINTS. DRAW ON A FACE, HAIR AND SHOULDERS WHEN THE PAINT IS DRY.

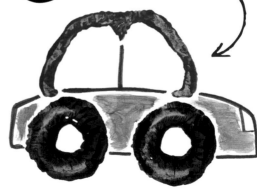

SPLAT-A-CATERPILLAR

PRINT THESE CUTE CATERPILLARS USING THE END OF A BALLOON!

1 Blow up a long balloon and knot the end. Hold on to the knot, dip the opposite end in some paint and press it on to paper. The harder you press, the bigger the printed blob will be.

2 Print a row of blobs to create a long or wiggly caterpillar. Dip the balloon in more paint each time. Press a bit harder to make the head bigger than the other blobs.

3 Paint two white spots on the head for eyes. When the paint is dry, draw on two black dots with a felt-tip pen.

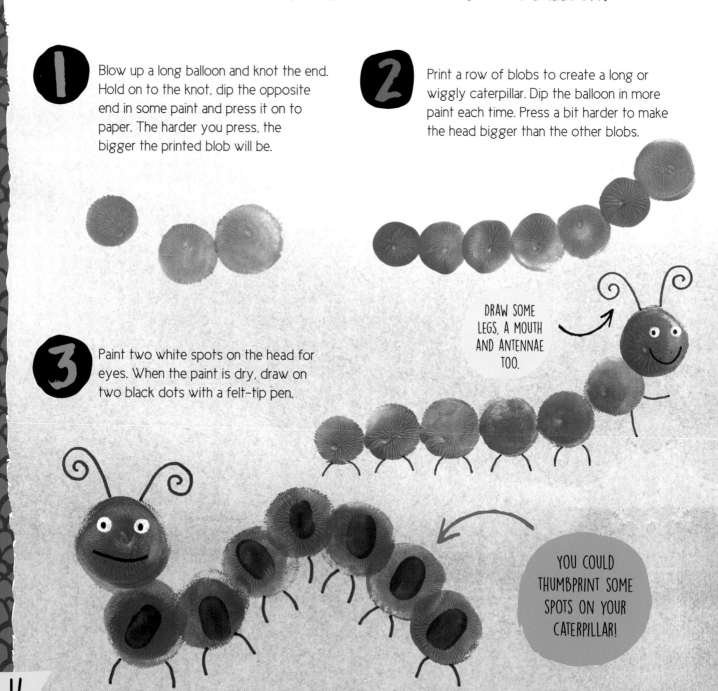

DRAW SOME LEGS, A MOUTH AND ANTENNAE TOO.

YOU COULD THUMBPRINT SOME SPOTS ON YOUR CATERPILLAR!

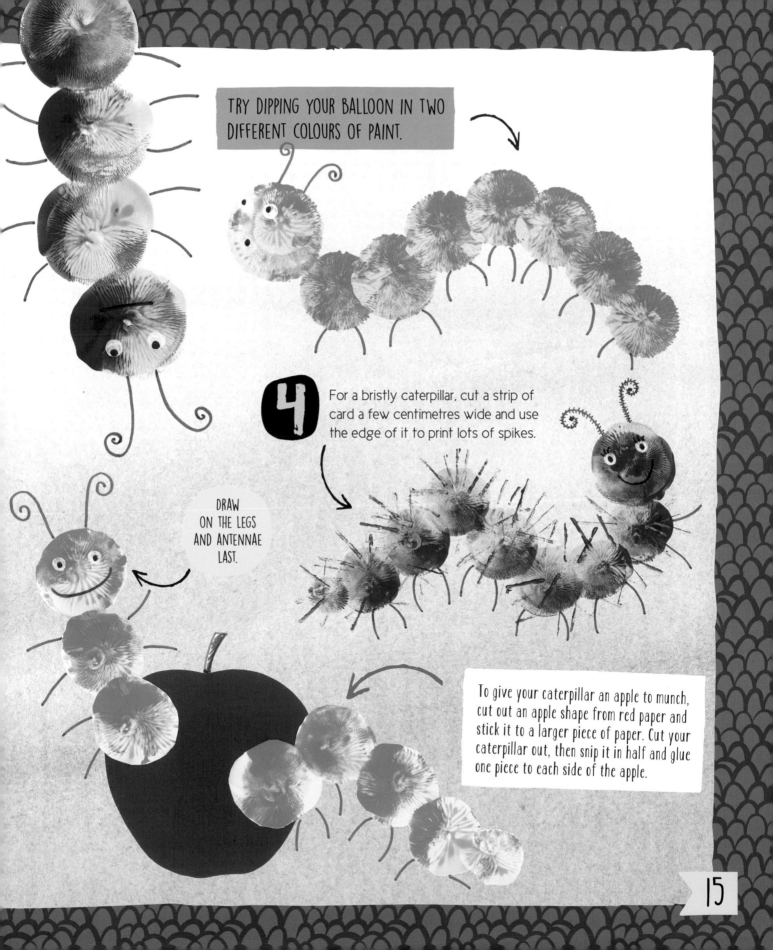

TRY DIPPING YOUR BALLOON IN TWO DIFFERENT COLOURS OF PAINT.

4 For a bristly caterpillar, cut a strip of card a few centimetres wide and use the edge of it to print lots of spikes.

DRAW ON THE LEGS AND ANTENNAE LAST.

To give your caterpillar an apple to munch, cut out an apple shape from red paper and stick it to a larger piece of paper. Cut your caterpillar out, then snip it in half and glue one piece to each side of the apple.

SPOTS AND STRIPES

THESE DANGLY DECORATIONS LOOK LOVELY HANGING ON A WALL.

 Draw a hen shape like the one below on to coloured card. Cut it out, then draw around it on some more card and cut out two more hen shapes. There are templates on p.30 to help you.

 Now decorate half of your shapes with spots and half with stripes. To make stripes, lay your cut-out on scrap paper. Cover the edge of a ruler in white paint, then press it across the cut-out. Repeat, spacing the lines a little apart.

HEN

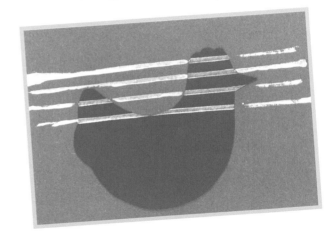

FOR EACH HEN, CUT OUT A WING AND AN EGG IN A DIFFERENT COLOUR.

WING

EGG

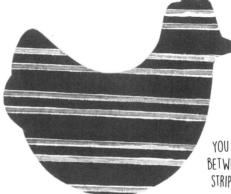

YOU COULD TRY DIFFERENT SPACES BETWEEN THE STRIPES, OR MAKE THE STRIPES GO FROM TOP TO BOTTOM.

For spots, print with the end of a pencil or the rim of a pen lid.

When everything is dry, glue a wing on to each hen. Draw on an eye and a line across the beak.

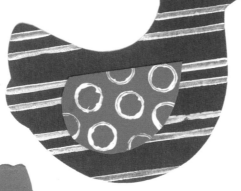

Make a loop at the top for hanging.

Lay your cut-outs face down in a line, with an egg below each hen. Cut a piece of wool, ribbon or string that reaches from top to bottom and tape it to the back of each shape.

Turn the shapes over and your dangly decoration is complete!

BUILDING BLOCKS

A SMALL STRIP OF CARDBOARD IS ALL YOU NEED TO DESIGN AND PRINT YOUR OWN BUILDING!

TO START:

Cut a strip of thick cardboard a few centimetres wide. Dip the edge of it in paint and practise printing with it on scrap paper.

CAN YOU BUILD A HOUSE?

PROJECT **1**

1. Print four lines to make a square – the sides could be one, two or even three strips long.

ONE PRINT MAKES A SHORT LINE LIKE THIS.

JOIN UP TWO PRINTS FOR A LONGER LINE.

2. Print the main walls first, then add a roof, windows, a chimney and a fence. For a door, drag the card strip sideways across the paper to pull the paint into a solid rectangle shape.

CAN YOU BUILD A TALL TOWER?

PROJECT **2**

1. Print three lines in a triangle shape at the top.

2. For battlements, cut a shorter strip of card. Print three sides of a square, then turn the corner, as shown.

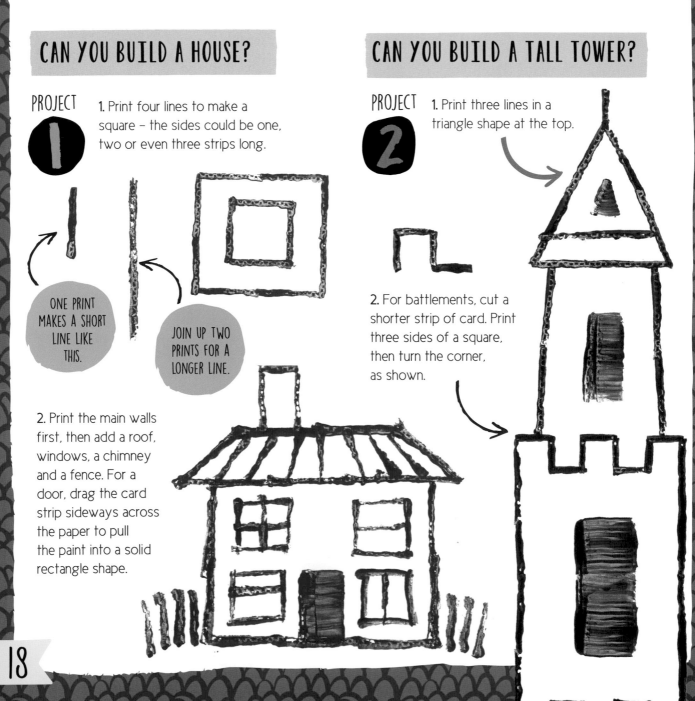

18

CAN YOU CREATE A CASTLE?

PROJECT **3**

To make a flag, drag your card strip across the paper in a zigzag.

FOR A FAIRY–TALE FEEL, YOU CAN USE WHITE PAINT ON COLOURED PAPER.

TRY PRINTING WINDOWS WITH THE SIDES OR ENDS OF A RUBBER.

PRINT LINES FOR A DRAWBRIDGE AND ADD SOME WATER BY DRAGGING THE CARD STRIP UP AND DOWN.

POTATO PARROTS

MAKE YOUR SPUDS SQUAWK AS YOU PRINT THESE PRETTY PARROTS! YOU'LL NEED TWO FAIRLY LARGE POTATOES.

1 Ask an adult to help you cut one potato in half lengthways to give a big, oval-shaped flat surface, and the other widthways to give a smaller oval. Dry the surfaces with kitchen paper.

Cover the large piece in yellow paint and print it on white paper. Cover the smaller piece in red paint and print it on top, like this.

2 Cut a wedge from the spare big piece of potato, and use it to print red wings and a tail.

3 When the prints are dry, paint a white face like this on to the parrot's head. Scratch some curved lines into the wet paint using the end of your paintbrush.

4 When the face is dry, paint on a black beak and eyes. You could add some red head feathers, and a grey line down the middle of the beak, too.

USE BROWN PAINT AND THE EDGE OF A STRIP OF CARD TO PRINT A BRANCH. PAINT SOME CLAWS CLINGING ON TO IT.

TO MAKE A FLYING PARROT, PRINT A FEW STRIPS ON EACH SIDE FOR FLAPPING WINGS, AND EXTRA STRIPS FOR THE TAIL.

IF YOU HAVE SOME OLD BROCCOLI, YOU COULD USE IT TO PRINT GREEN LEAVES!

THIS PINK CHEEK WAS MADE WITH A FINGERPRINT.

FOR A SIDEWAYS PARROT, PRINT THE WING STRIPS AT THE BACK ONLY.

MONSTER MADNESS

START WITH A SIMPLE FRUIT PRINT AND SEE WHAT CRAZY CREATURES YOU CAN MAKE!

1 Cut a piece of fruit in half, so that one side is flat. Dry the flat surface with kitchen paper, then cover it with paint and press it on to paper. Make a few prints, leaving space around each one.

ORANGE

PEAR

APPLE

2 While your prints are drying, cut out some shapes like these from coloured paper. Make them the right size for your prints.

MOUTH: STICK ON WHITE SHAPES FOR TEETH.

EYES: STICK A CIRCLE OF WHITE PAPER ON A LARGER COLOURED CIRCLE AND DRAW ON A BLACK DOT.

3 Glue the paper shapes to your prints to make monsters!

ARMS AND LEGS: CAN BE LONG OR SHORT, CLAWED OR WEBBED!

ANTENNAE

TAIL

SPIKES AND HORNS

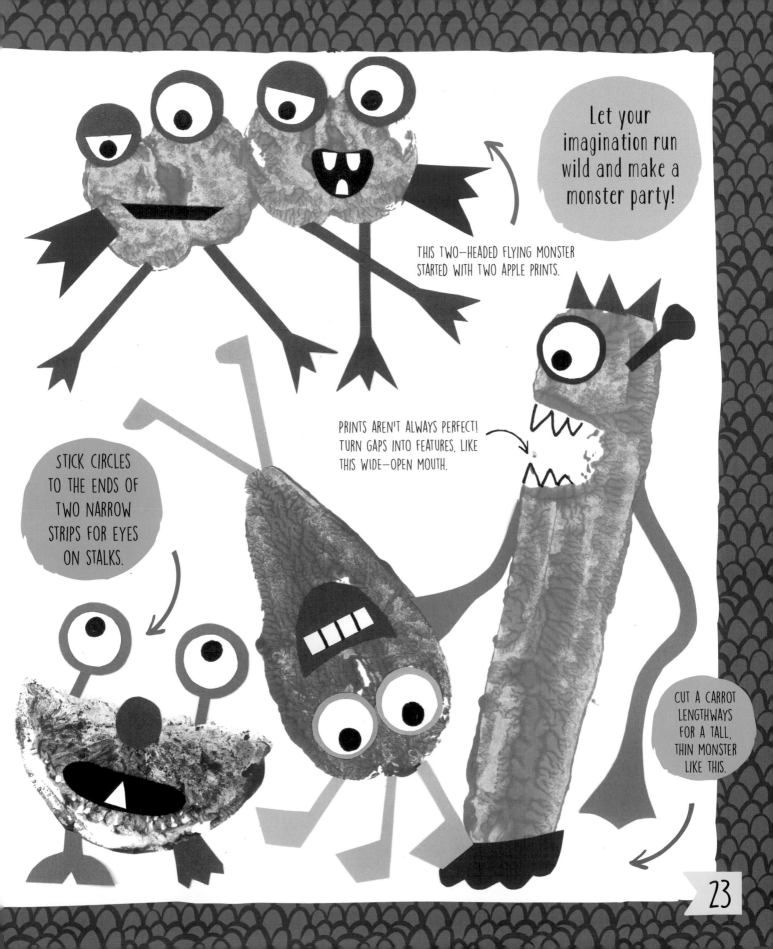

Let your imagination run wild and make a monster party!

THIS TWO-HEADED FLYING MONSTER STARTED WITH TWO APPLE PRINTS.

PRINTS AREN'T ALWAYS PERFECT! TURN GAPS INTO FEATURES, LIKE THIS WIDE-OPEN MOUTH.

STICK CIRCLES TO THE ENDS OF TWO NARROW STRIPS FOR EYES ON STALKS.

CUT A CARROT LENGTHWAYS FOR A TALL, THIN MONSTER LIKE THIS.

23

SPONGY WRAP

USE A TRIANGLE CUT FROM AN EVERYDAY SPONGE TO PRINT YOUR OWN WRAPPING PAPER.

1 Cut a triangle shape from a rectangular kitchen sponge. Dip this in paint and practise making prints with it like this:

FOUR TRIANGLES IN A CROSS SHAPE, OR FIVE TRIANGLES IN A STAR

TWO TRIANGLES WITH POINTS TOGETHER

TWO TRIANGLES WITH SIDES TOGETHER

FOUR TRIANGLES WITH POINTS IN THE MIDDLE

ROWS OF TRIANGLES

2 Now try repeating the pattern all over a sheet of paper. When it's dry, you can use it to wrap presents!

TEAR A SMALL PIECE OF SPONGE TO PRINT A BLOB IN THE MIDDLE OF A BOW.

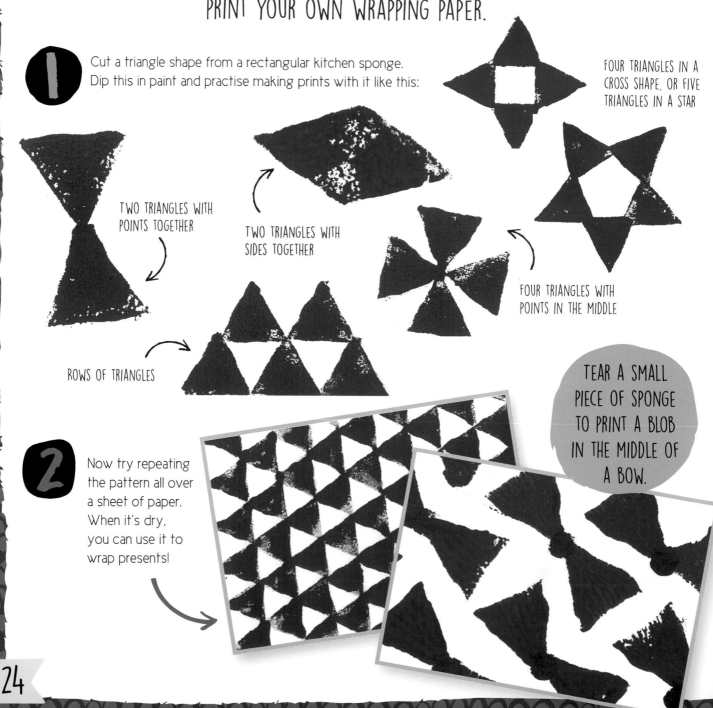

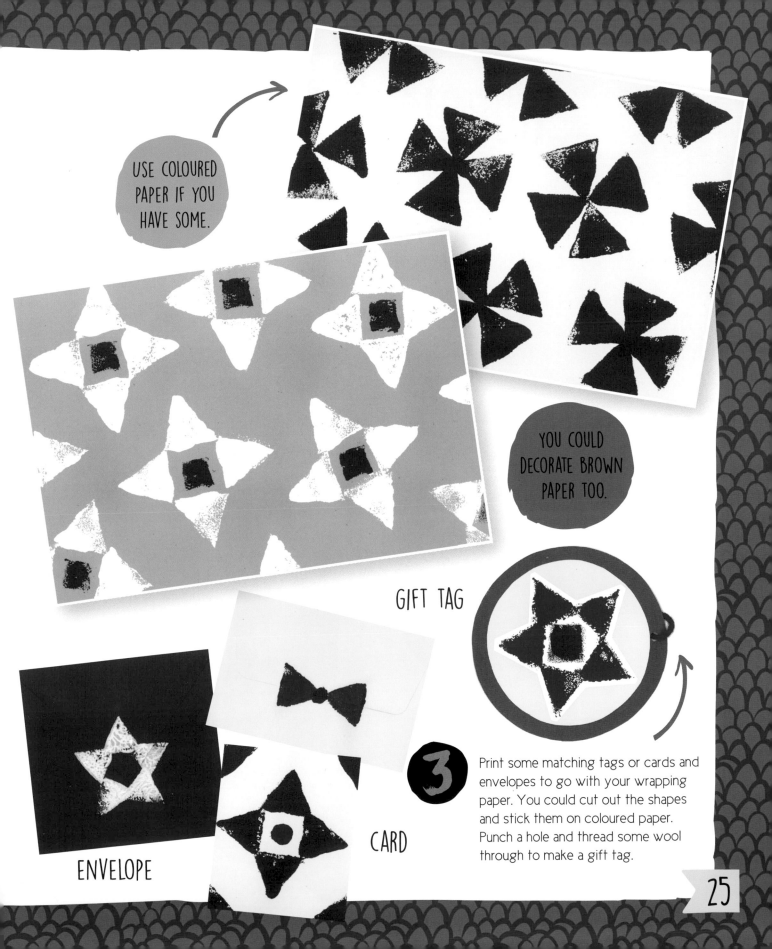

USE COLOURED PAPER IF YOU HAVE SOME.

YOU COULD DECORATE BROWN PAPER TOO.

GIFT TAG

ENVELOPE

CARD

3 Print some matching tags or cards and envelopes to go with your wrapping paper. You could cut out the shapes and stick them on coloured paper. Punch a hole and thread some wool through to make a gift tag.

25

BUBBLY SNAKES

PRINTING WITH BUBBLE WRAP IS A GREAT WAY TO MAKE SNAKY SCALES!

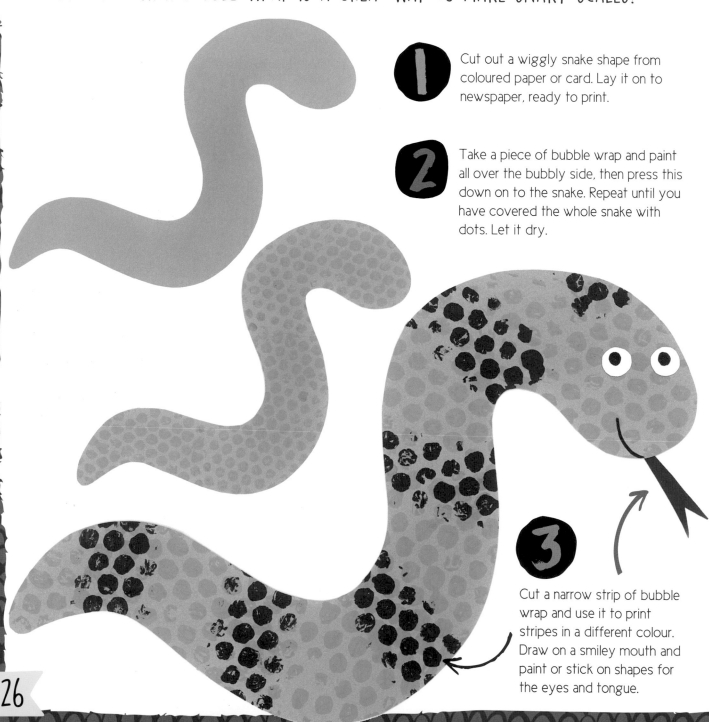

1 Cut out a wiggly snake shape from coloured paper or card. Lay it on to newspaper, ready to print.

2 Take a piece of bubble wrap and paint all over the bubbly side, then press this down on to the snake. Repeat until you have covered the whole snake with dots. Let it dry.

3 Cut a narrow strip of bubble wrap and use it to print stripes in a different colour. Draw on a smiley mouth and paint or stick on shapes for the eyes and tongue.

PRINT WITH A SMALL CIRCLE OF BUBBLE WRAP FOR A PATTERN LIKE THIS.

YOU COULD TRY MAKING A SLEEPY SNAKE! CUT A SPIRAL SHAPE FROM CARD AND PRINT IT USING BUBBLE WRAP AS BEFORE.

What other scaly reptiles can you print?

For this chameleon, use the templates on p.30 to draw the shape on coloured paper. Cut it out and print some bubble-wrap stripes. Use different coloured paper to make the legs, eye socket and spikes. Glue them on.

YOU COULD PRINT A GREEN BRANCH ON WHITE PAPER AND STICK THE CHAMELEON ON TOP!

27

STAMP INTO SPACE

SEND YOUR FOOTPRINT INTO ORBIT BY TURNING IT INTO A SPACE ROCKET!

1 You'll need a sheet of dark blue or black paper. Paint the bottom of your foot white, and your toes orange. Tread firmly on the paper, keeping your foot still to make a print. Lift your foot off carefully and wipe it clean.

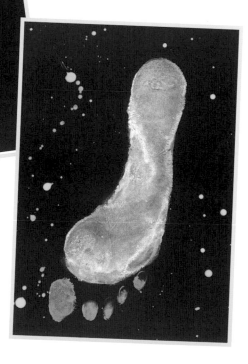

3 Cut out shapes like these from coloured paper. Make sure you make them the right size for your footprint.

2 When your footprint is dry, lay it on newspaper. Add a little water to some yellow paint in a cup. Use a paintbrush to splatter-paint some stars. Ideally do this outside!

4 Glue the paper shapes on to your rocket. In the porthole, make a thumbprint and draw on an astronaut's face.

5 To make a moon, draw a circle on to cardboard and cut it out. Sponge white paint unevenly all over it, then press it on to dark-coloured paper to make a print.

MAKE AN EARTH PRINT IN THE SAME WAY AS THE MOON, BUT USE A LARGER CARDBOARD CIRCLE AND ADD SOME WHITE AND GREEN PAINT TOO. PRINT IT ON TO LIGHT BLUE PAPER AND CUT IT OUT.

TEMPLATES

LEAFY LIONS
P.6–7

SPOTS AND STRIPES
P.16–17

BUBBLY SNAKES
P.26–27

VEGGIE JAM
P.12–13

GLOSSARY

OUTLINE a line showing the shape of an object

OVAL a rounded shape that is slightly longer than a circle, like an egg

PRINT to make an image by pressing a painted or inked object on to paper, card or another surface. The printed image comes out in reverse

SPLATTER-PAINT to dip a paintbrush in watery paint, then flick it over paper for a sprayed or splashed effect

STAMPING another word for printing with an object covered in paint or ink

TEMPLATE a shape used as a guideline to draw or cut around

ZIGZAG a line that bends at sharp angles from left to right